T0194497

The Balance of Life

The Happy Quotient:

How to Maintain a Happy and Successful Life

First Lady Dr. Amelia Jefferson

WESTBOW
P R E S S®
A DIVISION OF THOMAS NELSON
& ZONDERVAN

WestBow Press books may be ordered through booksellers or by contacting:

WestBow Press
A Division of Thomas Nelson & Zondervan
1663 Liberty Drive
Bloomington, IN 47403
www.westbowpress.com
1 (866) 928-1240

Because of the dynamic nature of the Internet, any web addresses or links contained in this book may have changed since publication and may no longer be valid. The views expressed in this work are solely those of the author and do not necessarily reflect the views of the publisher, and the publisher hereby disclaims any responsibility for them.

Any people depicted in stock imagery provided by Getty Images are models, and such images are being used for illustrative purposes only. Certain stock imagery © Getty Images.

THE HOLY BIBLE, NEW INTERNATIONAL VERSION®, NIV® Copyright © 1973, 1978, 1984, 2011 by Biblica, Inc.® Used by permission. All rights reserved worldwide.

Scripture taken from the New King James Version®. Copyright © 1982 by Thomas Nelson. Used by permission. All rights reserved.

Scripture quotations marked (NLT) are taken from the Holy Bible, New Living Translation, copyright © 1996, 2004, 2007 by Tyndale House Foundation. Used by permission of Tyndale House Publishers, Inc., Carol Stream, Illinois 60188. All rights reserved.

ISBN: 978-1-9736-7447-4 (sc)
ISBN: 978-1-9736-7446-7 (e)

Library of Congress Control Number: 2019913772

Print information available on the last page.

WestBow Press rev. date: 3/26/2020

Contents

"Everybody measures success in having a car, having a big house, but success is measured in your happiness cause if you ain't happy it don't mean a thing."

Quote by Martin Lawrence when he appeared on The Arsenio Hall Show (circa the 1990s)

Success Starts with Being Happy

I decided to write this book because so many people want to know the secrets of being successful. Success begins with being happy. I didn't think being happy was a big deal until people started to make comments about how happy I am all the time and how I am always smiling! Other comments I hear often are, "I know your husband spoils you!" and "You must not have any stress in your life!" It's very true that my husband spoils me but not having stress in my life is another story. Surprisingly, for many of my years, I have been tremendously stressed out with family, work, church and school. Even down to being depressed and having thoughts of suicide. However, no one knew the pains I suffered because I decided, in the end, to be happy regardless of my situation. I decided to examine my own life and share the secrets of being happy to help other people reach their God-given potential and live a happy life. Happiness is the foundation of being successful, compassionate, and caring. Secondly, I realized that people love to be around those who are positive and happy! As simple as it sounds, many of us are not happy. We

1

are not happy with our jobs, co-workers, church, pastor, wife, husband, children, family, how much money we have, where we live, our businesses, or anything else. We have glimpses of happiness; but, not overall happiness. I'm here to share with you that these are "real life" situations and there's no way around them. Life is not perfect. It's how you deal with these situations and your personal resilience that will help you regain your happiness.

As an educator, I always encourage my students to make good decisions impressing upon them that the decisions they make today will determine their future. As adults, we have had to suffer the consequences for making poor decisions that have affected our overall happiness. So how do we turn it all around and maintain a successful, happy, and compassionate life? Since you cannot rewrite the past, I will give you a few simple tools to use to maintain overall happiness.

As simple as it sounds, you have to choose to be happy. Yes, happiness is a choice! However, if you have a lot of drama or sadness in your life, it is difficult to make that choice. On the other hand, I have met remarkable men and women who have been abused, are fatherless or motherless, passed over for promotions, failed at love and business over and over again who still maintain a happy, positive attitude. What is their secret and how can you too be a champion over hardship? The secret is that they understand hardship, heartbreak, and disappointment are all a part of every human being's life. I love the saying that you're either "going through a storm, coming out of a storm, or on your way into one!"

No one is perfect. When people are hurting, stressed

and going through a storm, I always encourage them not to give up, but to keep going. No one said life will be easy. There are many pitfalls and challenges that we will have to overcome. Unfortunately, when we are going through the storm, we cannot see the light at the end of the tunnel. We feel stuck and defeated. Storms never last. When they are over, you're done. Once you're done, you can enjoy the fruits of your labor or learn a valuable lesson.

For example, let's say you're in graduate school. You have a full-time job and you are married with children. It's going to be difficult managing all of those responsibilities. Huge sacrifices will have to be made and the road will be long, but the outcome will not only benefit you, it will add value to the family as well. I suggest that you have a family meeting to discuss your personal goals. Let them know what you want to do. Tell them about the sacrifices you will have to make and how all of these actions will ultimately benefit them as well.

I've noticed that part of not being able to choose happiness is that our families make us feel guilty about achieving our goals. However, if we explain to them about what has to be done, include them in our goals/dreams, and makeup time with them when we have time available, they will become more understanding. Often times, we lack the ability to use communication as an effective way to prevent hardship.

Communication is also an effective way to get your point across to individuals who may have hurt you. We allow people to say things to us that deaden our spirit and we don't address them. We let the feeling continue to build until one day, we explode. Many times these people don't even realize they have hurt you. Additionally, if you told them that they hurt you, they would apologize and not perform those actions again. That's if they care about you. Some people will not be able to change because of their own unhappiness. This type of person you have to remove from your life. I always say, "if you're not adding to my life, you're a distraction." Unfortunately, when you have "life issues" going on, you don't need people in your life tearing you down. You need all that extra energy to refuel from the other issues in your life that are not easily exterminated.

Divine Intervention

"And we know that in all things God works for the good of those who love him, who have been called according to his purpose."

Romans 8:28 (NIV Version)

The next thing is to lead a spiritual life and to learn how to pray. It's a wonderful journey when you have a relationship with God and he reveals your purpose to you. Many of us do not have a purpose or a planned direction. I remember going to college feeling like I was supposed to know what I wanted to become when it was all said and done. Truthfully, I did not know. Once I graduated, I went in a completely different direction than my major field of study (Radio, TV & Film) which, in retrospect, I believe God had given me a gift of working behind the scenes and producing creative work. However, due to fear, I went into teaching. The gift of teaching was passed down to me by my mother and aunt. There is nothing wrong with teaching, I love it and I have touched many lives positively. What I'm trying to say is, even as young adults, we don't know what we want to do or where we want to go. Some of us follow the first course we fall into and others follow a close friend or family member into a profession that we never truly considered. That is why prayer is so important. Prayer allows your mind to clear out any distractions and connect with your soul to find answers to questions that your natural mind is unable to reach. I remember being frustrated at work because I felt overwhelmed at the variety of duties I had to perform and the long hours I put in. After praying for several weeks, God revealed to me that He was preparing me for a huge opportunity. This close encounter with God revealed my future path and allowed me to be happy and grateful for a future opportunity to run my own school or manage a District Department.

Notice that I said, "after praying for several weeks!" God does not reveal things to us when we want Him to reveal them. He will reveal them in His own time, not ours. Therefore, He might not answer you in a week or a month. It could take years! I don't know what His time frame is for you, but you have to keep praying until He answers you. While praying and asking God to reveal your purpose, make sure to thank God for the things that He has already given you, such as your job, business, family, food, necessities, and shelter. And some of these things may not make you happy, but God still likes to know that you appreciate what He has allowed you to have.

It always saddens me when I hear my co-workers or

friends complaining about their jobs. First of all, it's called a job for a reason! Unless you are truly working in your passion, you will not have a love affair with your work. During this time, the economy is still unstable. It has not fully rebounded from The Great Recession of 2008, which began December 2007 according to The National Bureau of Economic Research (NBER). So many companies are laying off hundreds and even thousands of people from their jobs; yet, we have the nerve to complain about the job we have. Thank you, Jesus, for allowing me to have a job! However, the blessing for some people is being laid off is what led them to their passion which has allowed them to become very successful and happy.

Praying is therapeutic. It's that "me time" everyone needs to keep their mind and body balanced. This is personal time with God, away from your family and friends, is where you can just have a conversation with your Heavenly Father. It's relaxing and it gives you a different perspective than your mind can conceive.

Meditation in the form of a Daily Word helps us keep life in perspective. There are some great publications you can order that use Bible verses in an everyday context. These are awesome stories that keep you captivated. The stories are usually short and some even include a prayer. The foundational idea is to pray after reading each scenario and ask God, "What lessons do you want me to learn from this story? How can I apply this lesson to my own life? Who can I uplift with this message by sharing this great information?"

The Balance of Life

"Be very careful, then, how you live—not as unwise but as wise"

Ephesians 5:15 (NIV Version)

Once your prayer life is solidified, it's time to balance your life. When I talk about "the balance of life," I'm speaking of keeping your life events at a level where they do not impact another area negatively. These life events include faith, work, family, friends, and organizations. Now, of course, your family and faith should be the center of your happiness; but, you have to make that determination.

It helps if you enjoy your job because if your job makes you happy, it becomes easy to provide for your family. Although your job is an important asset of balancing your life, it usually takes up 50 percent of your time. Therefore, it leaves you the remaining 50 percent to divide among your faith, family, friends, and other activities. In some scenarios, depending on the type of job, we spend more than 50 percent of our time working and negatively impacting the other areas of our lives. Therefore, it creates an environment where we are stressed out and unhappy. If this happens, we can find ourselves pulling away from our faith, family, friends, and other activities.

When things are not going well in our lives, our prayer life diminishes. Through my own experience as a pastor's wife, I know of situations where the pastor is so engrossed in his faith and his church congregation that the family becomes secondary. In this example, if the family is not happy because they are being ignored rather than placed as a high priority, guess what? The pastor won't be happy. It's a trickle-down and trickle-up effect. Additionally, this scenario happens when a parent exceeds their 50 percent at work and everyone else gets little time or no time at all.

In this chapter of the book, I really want to focus on "the balance of life" because I believe this is where a lot of unhappiness stems from. If we can get ahead of this phenomenon, we can be happy. We have to take a self-assessment of our lives to know where to begin. Look at the events in your life, write them down (Self-Assessment is located in the Appendix). Write underneath each event the percentage of time you spend on it. Do your results make you happy? Who do they impact? Don't leave out the most important event of life, and that's you! Taking care of yourself is key to your happiness.

Sometimes we put the happiness of others as a priority while destroying ourselves. For example, we might do something for someone not because we want to but because the person asks us to do it. It makes them happy while leaving us unhappy and empty or might even leave us feeling used! I'm not saying you shouldn't help out a friend or a family member. I am saying that your actions should not be at the expense of your happiness.

This is where many of us get caught in an endless cycle and we have to ask God for strength to break it! For example, if you loan money to a family member or friend and they do not pay you back, don't loan them any more money. We already know the failure to repay us will lead to negative feelings and cause feuds that can last for years. I don't understand why we continue to make decisions that we know will make us unhappy. Why do we continue to allow other people to make us unhappy? This is a variable that can be controlled. Unfortunately, if we continue down this path, we will self-destruct.

Low self-esteem is an enemy that keeps us unhappy. When we pray, we need to ask God to help us love ourselves and help us not depend on others to validate us! Unfortunately, low self-esteem is a lack of self-love. Many of us have childhood issues that have become adult issues causing us a life filled with unhappiness.

Many of us do not believe in seeking professional help to help us deal with our emotional issues. I remember being a shy, quiet student on the campus of Howard University. The campus was so large and students were always walking, talking, and hanging out on The Yard. I used to avoid people the best I could because I didn't like myself and I didn't think anyone else would like me either. I rushed across the campus to my classes with my head down. I hid in the library during my free breaks between classes. I hid behind myself until one day it all changed. I realized how great I was! I can't remember what led to my first discovery of self-worth, but it happened to me at Howard University! I came out of my shell and had a feeling of confidence and worth. I became engaged in campus life and met some long-time friends. My college experience helped to change my life! I loved myself and wanted to show love to others!

Even when I completed my graduate studies at Clark Atlanta University, one of my professors, Dr. Norman, asked me where did my self-love come from? I'll never forget it. He singled me out in class and asked, "Where do you get your confidence from?" It took me a minute to respond, so he followed up with another question. "Who do you love and admire in your family that has given you confirmation that counted?" After thinking about the question more deeply, I responded, "My dad!"

Just to give you all a little background about my dad, he is really my uncle (God rest his soul). My mom left Tupelo and moved to Chicago with her sister, her brother-in-law, and their two daughters. I was born and raised in my aunt and uncle's home in an extended family environment. Growing up, I heard my two cousins call their father "Daddy" so I adopted it and called him "Daddy" too!

The question from Dr. Norman and Rev. Thomas, later, revealed to me that for little girls, it is important to have a loving and positive relationship with their father. In my situation, it also proved that it doesn't have to be your biological father, but a father figure. So I was blessed with an awesome daddy (uncle) who loved and cared for me and thought that I was the most beautiful girl in the world. As a child, I would sit on his lap for hours while he watched TV and talked on the phone. He became the standard of what I searched for in my husband.

Ladies, you must select a loving and caring man for you and your children because it will have a positive effect on your children. I'm not saying that you have to know everything about rearing children, but do some reading and research to make sure that your children get a loving, supportive, and balanced childhood. If that means going to the internet to look up information, then that's what you have to do! Nowadays, there's no excuse not to know!

Finally, if you know someone who has done a great job raising their children, spend some time with them to soak up as much information as possible. Raising children is the most difficult job, but it's also the most important.

Happiness begins in childhood! For women especially, if we have a positive relationship with our fathers, the more self-worth we will generate! Now, if you don't have a positive relationship with your father, you have to do a couple of things to get your happy back! The first thing is to forgive your father for the lack of love and support he gave you as a child and/or as a young woman. Secondly, love him for who he is, not who you expect him to be. Many women have an idea of who they want their father to be or who they think he should be. They look to TV dads like Mike Brady, Philip Banks, Ward Cleaver, Andy Griffith or Rev. Run as the ideal father. They also look to the fathers of their friends to help formulate their perception of what a great dad is. Unfortunately, this causes frustration and unhappiness. If you won't accept your father for who he is and all his faults, you will never gain true happiness.

Having Positive Relationships

"I have told you these things, so that in me you may have peace. In this world, you will have trouble. But take heart! I have overcome the world."

John 16:33 (NIV Version)

Your happy quotient improves the chances of having positive relationships with loved ones. Stress can progress greatly when you are constantly upset about what someone said or did to you. Especially when you have feelings of being disrespected or someone was just mean-spirited. The best way to combat negative relationships is to confront the problem head-on. Many times, when people hurt our feelings, we dismiss the offense! However, it continues to fester inside and when another situation arises, we lose it! I have learned from experience that many people do not intentionally try to hurt your feelings. It could come from the person's culture, upbringing or ignorance. However, some individuals do intentionally try to push you to your limits.

As a school leader, it is especially difficult to motivate staff and encourage them at the same time without hurting their feelings. When I was a school administrator, at the beginning of the year, I reminded teachers that if I said something to offend them or hurt their feelings, to please come discuss it with me. I had a tendency to say things a little too straightforward. However, my straightforwardness comes from a place of love and concern to motivate and challenge people. Trust me, I have worked very hard on saying things gentler because I can always hear my sister in my ear making me promise not to be rude to folks. Honestly, to me, I'm not being rude, I just have great expectations that might come off as being rude. It's the observation of an outsider looking in to tell you to "up your game!" Though it is coming from a loving and encouraging place, I have had to learn to soften the way I speak to people because I realize certain people are very sensitive.

I can remember my excitement when my co-workers came to tell me that I offended them or upset them with something I said in a faculty meeting. Of course, I had no malice in my heart nor was my intent to hurt their feelings. So we talked about it and I apologized. Then I made sure not to make those same mistakes again. I gave this example because you can walk around for days, weeks, or even years carrying around what someone said or did that hurt you and the same person doesn't even realize it. I always give people the benefit of the doubt by trying to search for reasons why certain things are said.

Once you get to know someone, you learn about their cultural attitude which is behavior based on perceptions learned through family and experiences.

Creating positive relationships with family is probably the most difficult. It's funny how siblings grow up in the same house, have the same parents and end up being so different. Even sometimes our parents get so unhappy and overwhelmed with family, they opt for divorce. Unfortunately, divorce impacts the children negatively.

I remember in the "golden" years, husbands and wives stayed together for the children. It was an important American family value to stay together for the children even though the relationship was emotionally over. Around 50% of all marriages in the United States end in divorce and the number is similarly high in many other developed nations (McKinley Irvin Family Law Website Posted October 30, 2012). The best way to create a loving, caring and happy atmosphere for children is to stay married and present a positive relationship example around your children. Children need both parents to create a stable home with love and affection.

If divorce is inevitable, both parents have to equally show care and concern for the children by remaining on the same page. It's more difficult to maintain a united front if parents are no longer married. Unfortunately, if the divorce resulted in hurt feelings, children will try to manipulate their parents. One way children use the separation is by pitting one parent against the other. On the other hand, parents will use their children to hurt the other parent like they were hurt in the separation of the relationship. This could be in the form of talking negatively about the parent, pointing out things the other parent promised to do and didn't, or things the parent is not doing at all and should be doing. As a result of these behaviors, children become emotionally scarred adults who continue this cycle with their children. A successful step-parent once shared this nugget of information, "You can't tell a child or point out to a child how bad the other parent is (even when you know they are terrible). You have to let them find out on their own." This transition is a better one for a healthy childhood than degrading the parent.

Secondly, people might be surprised to know that deferred gratification is the key to happiness. My aunt used to always tell me, "Don't try to keep up with the Joneses!" As I became older, I realized that some people try to compete with their family members, neighbors, and/or friends only to find themselves in a depressed cycle. When you obtain things by copying what others have acquired, happiness only lasts for a short period before you end up breaking the bank, or sacrificing other things that make you happy so you can continue to keep up with others. If there is something you want, especially if it's expensive, plan for it. Do the research. Find out what additional costs are associated with ownership. I promise it will alleviate the stress and your happy quotient will increase. Many times, when we buy costly items, we don't factor additional costs. For example, if you buy a new house that's bigger than your last house, all of the expenses will increase. With more square footage, your utilities and maintenance cost increase. So while you're only thinking about the house note, don't forget to add those additional costs in your future monthly budget. On the other hand, if you waited and planned for the additional costs, you will be happier in the long run even if the gratification is deferred.

Also, even with smaller items, we need to be cautious. Keeping up with the current fashion trends and the latest technology can break the bank. This constant need to have the latest of the latest will leave you broke and controlled by debt. This will lower your happy quotient. Start challenging your mind to shop smarter and defer getting items when they first come out.

If you are fortunate enough to find a loving partner, they can help add balance to your life. Hopefully, the two of you have different strengths and weaknesses that together will make you unbeatable! For example, I like to shop and spend money. My husband doesn't like to shop and he'd rather save money. Can you imagine if we both liked to shop and spend money? Yes, you guessed it, we would be broke and homeless! I know you think that your partner should be compatible and share common characteristics; but, look for someone who can complete you. If you are unorganized, you need to find someone who is organized. If you can't cook, look for someone who loves cooking. This way, it's a true partnership where you complete each other and your happy quotient increases.

Giving Back

Then he said to his disciples, "The harvest is plentiful but the workers are few."

Matthew 9:37 (NIV Version)

What is extremely satisfying is the ability to give back. It brings me so much joy when I can help others. Helping others is one of my gifts! I really enjoy it and it increases my happy quotient.

Giving back can be done in several ways. Look into your heart and find out where your passion lies. It might be mentoring young girls, assisting senior citizens, caring for babies, teaching college students how to budget their money, or helping to transition homeless families into steady homes. Wherever your heart lies, many organizations can help you accomplish these goals or you can start your own as a "one-man show." You would be surprised by how many individual volunteers I have met at my school. They stop by or call offering to help. They want to give away school supplies and clothes, or they want to read to the children or give a presentation to introduce students to new career opportunities. Schools, hospitals, churches, prisons, and senior citizen's facilities are always in need of volunteers and it helps to fill a void that would otherwise be missing.

Giving back is so easy! You can stop by a local facility or you can Google one. Either way, helping others is very rewarding and the recipients are always so appreciative. Now you might not be able to volunteer every day or even once a week, but it's called volunteer work for a reason. There is really no set agenda unless you want one.

When you visit the facility, get the name of who is in charge of volunteers so they can get you started right away. Now if you're not a people person, just let the volunteer coordinator know so they can put you to work with limited person-to-person interaction. Therefore, don't allow this character trait to keep you from helping others. You will be amazed at how much work needs to be done behind the scenes and how happy you will become.

Setting Realistic Goals

"Suppose one of you wants to build a tower. Won't you first sit down and estimate the cost to see if you have enough money to complete it?"

Luke 14:28 (NIV Version)

In order to raise our happy quotient, we have to set realistic goals. Too many times we set ourselves up for failure and disappointment when we have high expectations that are not aligned with our ability or level of sacrifice. Speaking honestly, sometimes we set unrealistic goals that just don't make sense. For example, many people have an ideal viewpoint about marriage. Some of us believe when we get married everything will be perfect. All of the problems we experienced before we got married will suddenly disappear. Our spouse will be perfect, our home, and our children will all be perfect. We will have no problems and we will live out our lives in pure happiness. As you read that, you probably thought, *this is an imaginary world*, but some couples think this way about marriage. They even go as far as thinking that marriage will solve all of their issues. I wish marriage was a "magic pill," but it's not. However, if you understand that marriage is a partnership (meaning it takes two) between two people, you can frame your goals about marriage more realistically. Whenever you bring two strangers together, problems will arise especially when there are major differences between you like religion, how you each manage money and beliefs about how to raise children. Think about it, marriage brings together two people who either lived by themselves or with parents and other family members. They have been socialized to do things a certain way, the "family way." This immediately causes social conflict. Then adding to this social conflict is the difference in culture and religion. Many times when we fall in love, we don't even think about our partner's culture or religion. Unfortunately, this provides additional stress to relationships. When I talk to young couples about marriage, I always use the analogy that a marriage is similar to a job. It is challenging and rewarding at the same time; however, if you don't work on it, you'll lose it. Therefore, differences are eminent and compromise is essential.

Finally, when you add children to the equation, it becomes even more complex. However, if you understand that differences will occur and you're a reasonable person, getting over different challenges will improve your happy quotient. I love when couples joke about their differences. It's a way to make the situation light and have some fun while doing it. Couples don't have to be serious all the time. Have fun and turn those negative situations in to fun times.

While you're dating your significant other, have open communication about culture, religion, finances, and raising children. This way, you get an understanding of how this person thinks and what he or she values. These differences are not deal breakers, but know that some serious compromising must take place on behalf of both parties. You don't have to have a huge disagreement about everything. Also, don't bother about the little things. Save the partnership challenges for the large, meaningful battles. I suggest the implementation of a yearly family meeting (I have included a Family Meeting Agenda in the Appendix). This meeting is an opportunity to discuss the current situation and the development of family goals. Some couples may want to add a mid-year meeting just to follow up on a few family goals.

In my own life, family meetings have been very productive. We use our family meetings to list all of our expenses and split the responsibility of expenses. We also talk about family issues that we hardly ever talk about in everyday life, but that needs to be addressed. We also set a realistic goal on a plan to pay off credit card debt. We use our vacation time after New Year's Eve to have our yearly family meeting. This is the best way to start the New Year!

Let's look at another example. You want to lose 20 pounds by your birthday, but you like to eat unhealthy foods, your schedule is crazy, and you're allergic to exercise. By doing a self-assessment, this goal is not realistic for you!

In order to raise your happy quotient, opt for goals that are realistic and attainable. Try to change your diet and lose five pounds, then celebrate over that accomplishment. Later, add in exercise and celebrate that accomplishment.

If you have huge goals, try setting smaller ones first. As you celebrate those small milestones on your way to the larger goal, you will increase your happy quotient tremendously.

Being Your "Real Self"

"Am I now trying to win the approval of human beings, or of God? Or am I trying to please people? If I were still trying to please people, I would not be a servant of Christ."

Galatians 1:10 (NIV Version)

This chapter will begin to dig deep about what we think of ourselves and how we want other people to view us. I think it's safe to say that we all have insecurities. The key is how we deal with those insecurities and how we relate to other people will increase our happy quotient. If we can have a positive outlook toward life, have a sense of gratitude and motivation to improve ourselves, we can be happy.

Many of us are socialized by our family and surroundings. Meaning, we learn some negative habits (like lying) from our family and our environment. Some of us even use these negative habits as a mechanism to combat insecurities. However, it's only a quick fix and will eventually lead to anxiety. For example, if you put forth an image of riches, yet everywhere you go, you need help paying the bill or are unable to go to a variety of places where your friends go, this will eventually cause sadness because you're trying to live up to the false you which only exists at the moment. Or you end up in huge credit card debt trying to live out the image that you have falsely portrayed. Trust me, when the credit card companies come calling, it will be a source of stress and anxiety, therefore further reducing your happy quotient.

I think this is the most difficult attribute because it means we have to take an honest assessment of ourselves and some of the issues we don't want to deal with. For example, I used to go through money so quickly (I still do, but I've gotten better) and I wouldn't even look at my bank account because I didn't want to take ownership of my shortcomings. Many of us think if we avoid or ignore our issues, God will just whisk them away. When in actuality, they become a greater distraction that eventually destroys the happy quotient. Even as a married woman, I noticed that we don't want to deal with the deep issues that could really increase our happy quotient. Instead, we deal with surface issues where everyone can feel happy. What about later? Trust me, you might feel a sense of happiness and security at the moment, but those deep issues will resurface, if not tackled, and they will destroy your happy quotient. I know it's hard having those deep and hurtful conversations but after the hurt, joy returns. You feel a sense of relief.

For some of us, the most difficult action is change.

Change is hard, but a true change takes place on the inside of us. Our hearts and minds have to change. Some people say it's impossible to change. I'm here to say you can change; however, it is a process that won't happen overnight. It has to start from within and then you have to be courageous enough to align your actions with your changed mind.

I always tell people I'm a realist. No matter how bad it looks, I face my issues head-on and begin making a change. In some instances, you might need a support group, accountability group, counseling group, or discipleship group. The members of the groups are here to challenge you and hold you accountable to what you promised yourself. If the group is supporting your negative behavior, that's not your support group. They are enablers. We have to know the difference. If no one is challenging you, making you think deeper and move quicker, you are surrounded by enablers. Some of us like to keep enablers around because they keep our heads in the clouds. They prevent us from doing self-assessments, looking at ourselves deeply and making the necessary changes that will increase our happy quotient. Instead, we rather sit around and wonder why we're not happy and blame other people for our unhappiness. And, yes, your enabler(s) will usually be close family and friends. And, yes, they are the worst when it comes to your inner change. They consistently agree with you and ignore your bad actions. In the business realm, they have been called "yes men." I've heard from very successful people who said they didn't want "yes men" around them. They wanted people on their team who would challenge them and stretch their creative thinking. In other words, every successful person, business or organization will have some conflict. Always consider the source when considering where the conflict is coming from. Ask yourself, does this person have my best interest in mind, do they love and care for me, are they contributing positively to my life or the overall health and wealth of my company? Then, that person is needed to balance your actions. This is another example why you need divine intervention (reread this Chapter). The Holy Spirit will also help you recognize divine people but you have to be connected to God.

Overall Health

"Nevertheless, I will bring health and healing to it; I will heal my people and will let them enjoy abundant peace and security."

Jeremiah 33:6 (NIV Version)

Health is very important. The New Living Translation Bible says, "Don't you realize that your body is the temple of the Holy Spirit, who lives in you and was given to you by God? You do not belong to yourself," 1 Corinthians 6:19. Therefore, your body is a special place and should be handled with care. Unfortunately, when you don't take care of your body, it will begin to break down either due to neglect or illness.

I had the opportunity to take a nutrition class at my church sponsored by Lemell McMorris. It was amazing to see how bad we eat and how lazy we have become. Many of us can come off of prescription drugs just by exercising regularly and eating right. But we don't do it! We have excuses when we're feeling good, "Foods don't taste right unless they're fried." "I can't exercise, I might sweat out my hair," or "I can't exercise because my knee hurts." "I can't buy organic food because it's too expensive." Either you make positive changes to live a healthy lifestyle now or you will pay for it later. Do you think eating right is expensive? Wait until you see the doctor bills you'll have if you don't eat right.

I'm not saying that it will be easy. Trust me, I love to eat! Growing up, my meals consisted of cornbread on every plate, fried fish on Fridays and fried chicken on another day of the week. How about those sugary drinks that we love to drink like sodas, juices, wine, and energy drinks? Unfortunately, I just read an article revealing that diabetes is on the rise. At my sorority's volunteer service project, I had my blood sugar tested and it was high. Not to mention all the carbohydrates we love to eat that breakdown into sugar once it's digested. What about all of the packaged foods we love to eat? It's difficult, but we have to start sacrificing and changing our attitude towards food.

Isn't it amazing that all we need to do is change our diet? In Europe, they eat small meals while we like to "upsize it," "give me the biggest piece of chicken," or "give me the meal with the largest portion." And American food companies give us what we want. They pump our food with all types of steroids so the meat is "bigger." They put so much sugar and fillers in foods to make it taste so good that the addictive property in sugar keeps you going back again and again. Meats, fruits, and vegetables look perfect because unhealthy additives are added to make food appear perfect and give food longer shelf life. Successful restaurants serve large portions and our fast food chains offer biggie size and supersize.

Once you become knowledgeable about how food is manufactured, packaged, and distributed, it will change your mind about how you eat. Here's my recommendation on how to start eating healthy. Think about how you can begin to reduce your sugar intake. You can take out, replace, or reduce the frequency of how much you eat it. Start small! Think about two items you can change using the options above. For example, I stopped drinking soda altogether and changed my deep-fried foods to air fried, then reduced the number of times I eat fried foods.

As you get this first round of things under control, change something else. Start exercising by walking, then jogging, then running. Join a work out class at the gym, senior facility, or hospital. Start a workout group at work, work out in the mornings before work or after work. Hire a personal trainer or workout at home. I always say, there's no excuse not to work out when you can pull up workout routines on your cell phone, tablet or TV for free. They have a sports and fitness channel available 24-hours a day, 7 days a week.

Let's say you have bad knees and feet, guess what? There are tons of chair exercises that you can perform sitting in a chair (check out Chair-A-Cising by Daryl Madison). Once again start with 15 minutes (twice a week) and build up to an hour in time, then add more days. I think the biggest mistake people make is trying to go "hard in the paint." They start working out every day for an hour, then when they miss a day, "It's a wrap!" Try to build a workout routine in your life that works for you and your schedule to maintain for the rest of your life. For example, I work out twice a week. It works out well for my schedule because if I miss a day I can always make it up. Of course, I need to work out three times a week, it just doesn't work well with my schedule of work and other activities I'm involved in. In the past, twice a week was fine because half of the activities I participate in require me to move. However, now that my job is sedentary, I have begun to walk around my building or walk on the treadmill in our wellness center once or twice a week. At this time, I have to share with you the ideal "work out schedule is to perform strength training three times per week from thirty to forty minutes on non-consecutive days (Monday, Wednesday & Friday). This "work out" schedule includes a warm up and cool down. However, if you enjoy cardio, you can use cardio for your warm up and cool down for your strength training sessions. Ultimately, this should be your workout goal.

When changing to a happier and healthier lifestyle, you will need some type of motivation, especially if you are not self-motivated. Here are some suggestions. Start a team where everyone holds each other accountable and gives accolades for those who are consistent in meeting their goals. Have a "biggest loser contest." Purchase a Fitbit or download a similar app to your phone. Connect with other groups via churches, organizations, online communities, and health clubs. Reward yourself for meeting your goals. If you work out twice a week for several months, reward yourself. The bottom line is when you feel better, you exude happiness.

In addition to eating healthy and exercising regularly,

take care of personal hygiene in other areas such as teeth, hair, and nails. Do you have regularly scheduled appointments to see your dentist and primary care doctor? You need a team of professionals to stay healthy. Being healthy does not exclude you from illnesses. Healthy people get cancer and other illnesses, too. However, if you are in tune with your body and get regular check-ups, it can be caught early. When it's caught early, it's treatable.

Put Your Happy On

"The LORD has done it this very day; let
us rejoice today and be glad."

Psalm 118:24 (NIV Version)

This is probably my favorite chapter because this activity is so simple and easy. Have you ever wondered why people attach themselves emotionally to songs or pictures? It's because these things increase your happy quotient abundantly. Is there a song, poem, picture, movie, scripture, quote, or even a video clip from social media that makes you happy? Does it bring about a feeling that you can't get enough of so you play it or look at it multiple times? Amazingly, something so simple will bring you such joy. Once you find a mood shifter you enjoy, play it when you're feeling sad. And guess what? You can play it or read it over and over again.

Is there a hobby that you enjoy? For example, my favorite hobby is getting a hot stone massage. Out of all the different types of massages, the hot stone is my favorite. It relaxes me and puts me in a state of peace, happiness, and relaxation. It's so good that once I'm done, I can't get off the table right away. I have to lie on the table until I get feeling back in my body to move.

What is it that makes you happy? Is it shopping, exercising, reading magazines, or a hobby? There could be many things that provide the feeling of happiness and you can easily add these things to your schedule. I keep certain pictures in my phone that I can look at to change my mood in an instance. They bring me so much happiness and joy and they have the power to change my mood immediately.

Appendix I

The Balance of Life
Weekly Self Assessment
Sample Chart

Life Events	YOU Cycle 3hrs	FAITH Church 5hrs	HOME Family 5hrs	WORK DCSD 45hrs	CLUBS/ ORGANIZATIONS AKA	FREE	OTHER Business 5hrs
% Time Spent	5%	5%	5%	50%	5%	25%	5%
Priority Level	3	2	5	5	3	3	3

Directions - % Time Spent Weekly Category – Add up the total time you spend in a day (the time you spend awake, ex. 17 hours). Then calculate that number per week (17 X 5 = 85). Use this weekly number of hours to fill in the percentage for each life event category (Ex. If I work 45 hours per week, 45/85 = 0.529 X 100 = 52.941 Round to 50% to make it easier). The numbers should total 100%.

Then use the numbers 1 through 5 (5 being the highest priority) to rank each life event priority (Ex. WORK is a high priority, so it gets a ranking of 5). If you need more detail, you can place the specific name under each category title (see the table above under WORK).

Here is a blank chart for you.

Chart A

Life Events	YOU	FAITH	HOME	WORK	CLUBS/ ORGANIZATIONS	FREE	OTHE
% Time Spent							
Priority Level							

Chart B

Life Events	YOU	FAITH	HOME	WORK	CLUBS/ ORGANIZATIONS	FREE	OTHEF
Happy Quotient							
Priority Level							
Overall Rating							

Directions – Take the Priority Level Ratings and move them to Chart B. I want you to be able to look at the priority ratings in two scenarios. Use the numbers 1 – 5, 5 being the greatest and assign your ranking number for each category as it relates to the Happy Quotient and Impact Level. After you have completed the chart, add the total numbers to get the overall rating for each category. It will reveal what makes you the happiest, with the highest impact and priority. Now, you can rank them to see the top three categories. Do you agree? Now, it's time to analyze the charts (see information below).

Important Notes
- ✓ You do not have to have data in every category.
- ✓ You may assign the same rating numbers to multiple categories.
- ✓ You can ask yourself the following questions:
    - How happy does it make me feel?
    - What is the impact level on my life?
    - Is it a high priority?
    - Does it impact my family negatively (this would be a low number)?

Appendix II

The Balance of Life
Chart Analysis

After you have listed all of your jobs and activities and given them an overall rating, it's time to analyze the charts. Look closely at the results. Start looking at the rankings. Ask yourself the following questions:

Which activities make me happy?
What is the priority level?
How much time does it take?
Am I spending too much time on this activity?
Is it benefiting the family?
What things can I take out that will increase my happy quotient?
What can I add that will increase my happy quotient?
Is it a possibility to reduce the time spent on a low priority activity?
Do I see anything that sticks out?

Appendix III

The Balance of Life
Goals

Then list three goals that you would like to put in place to increase your happy quotient and balance your life. Work toward the goals and revisit the charts in three-to-six months. Have you made any changes? How close are you to your goals? Make adjustments and revisit the charts in three-to-six months. Ask yourself the same questions listed above.

HAPPY QUOTIENT GOALS

1.   Complete by _____
2.   Complete by _____
3.   Complete by _____

Appendix IV

Family Meeting Agenda

Goal Setting

- **Goal #1**   **Complete by_____**
- **Goal #2**   **Complete by_____**
- **Goal #3**   **Complete by_____**

Budget Plans

- **Financial Picture (includes salary, expenses, credit card debt, loan debt)**
- **Budget (How can we improve our household budget? What can we cut out our budget? What can we pay off? What can we refinance? What investments can we make?)**
  - **Emergency Savings Account**

Estate Planning

- Living Will
- Life Insurance
- Trust Funds
- Beneficiary Designations
- Powers of Appointment
- Property Ownership
- Gift
- Business Succession
- Retirement (Work & Additional)
- Current Investments
- Future Investments
- Research & Evaluation of these Investments

Spiritual Growth

- Family Prayer & Meditation
- Scripture Reading & Studying
- Family Worship (Church Home)

Relationship Growth

- Date Night(s)
- Family Vacations
- Family Events
- Family Activities

Family Issues

- Spouse
- Children

- Parents
- Friends

Open Topics

- What's on your mind that has not been covered in the family meeting?

Next Steps

- _____
- _____
- _____
- _____
- _____

Conclusion

"He will have no fear of bad news; his heart is steadfast, trusting in the Lord." Using the gifts God has given you, step out and take a risk-based on faith, trusting Him for success. If you do, "You will have good success" (Jos 1:8 NKJV).

Many times we overload ourselves unaware of the stress and sadness that it causes. I wrote this book to help people with active lives learn how to balance their activities. We also tend to take on too many commitments outside of family and our "normal" workload. Once you use, The Balance of Life Assessment, you can analyze your activities and make some decisions on how to reduce or add the time towards activities or take them out completely. I can not tell you which activities are important because every individual is unique. However, I added the "Other" Category because when I took the self-assessment myself, I didn't want to put my doctor visits in the category of "You." I wanted the "You" Category to be dedicated to things we do for ourselves that would help inspire, relax, and rejuvenate us. Although my doctor visits are a priority, I wanted them in a separate category.

Secondly, happiness is a choice. Even when you are

experiencing sadness, it's never too late to get your "happy back." It's what we do when we get knocked down. It's learning how to have thick skin and not take everything so personally. It's about learning how to say "no" and be happy with your decision. It's being able to keep a laser focus on the important things in life that will make us happy and give us the energy to complete the other tasks. We all need a balance and I pray that the Balance of Life Assessment will help you evaluate your life and motivate you to make positive changes.

Appendix V

The Balance of Life
Citations

John 16:33, **New International Version (NIV)**

Holy Bible, New International Version®, NIV® Copyright ©1973, 1978, 1984, 2011 by Biblica, Inc.® Used by permission. All rights reserved worldwide.

Cultural Attitudes Definition – Perceptions learned through family socialization that influences behavior where your experiences shape your ideologies and philosophies. (Barone and Blumenfield-James, 1998)

About the Author

First Lady Dr. Amelia Jefferson's educational and spiritual philosophy stems from her personal background, educational experiences and professional development. As a child, she was heavily influenced by her mother and aunt who were both teachers for the Chicago Public School System for more than 30 years. She earned a Bachelor of Arts Degree in Communications from Howard University, a Masters Degree in Urban Education from Concordia University, and a Specialist and Doctorate in Educational Leadership from Clark Atlanta University where she graduated with honors and was invited to become a Charter Member of Kappa Delta Pi International Honor Society.

Her professional background as an educator has taught her many life skills that she wants to share with others. She served as a teacher, gifted liaison, assistant principal and coordinator for the DeKalb County School District. In these rolls, First Lady has continued to support student academic success by carrying out the overall mission of the premier DeKalb County School District.

First Lady is an active member of Alpha Kappa Alpha Sorority, Inc. where she serves on a variety of committees. As an active member, she continues her mission to improve social and economic conditions through the sorority's community service programs.

First Lady is also a Registered Representative specializing in estate planning, wealth building and investments. She is a member of FINRA and has licenses in Life Insurance and Securities.

Finally as a wife to a pastor, First Lady Dr. Jefferson is an active member of Kingdom Fellowship Christian Church in Decatur, GA where she continues to internalize the central messages found throughout the bible. Her strong belief in God has allowed her to maintain a positive attitude through adversity. First Lady serves faithfully on a variety of ministries including the Women's Ministry, Choir, Youth and Young Adult Ministry and the Continuing Education Ministry. First Lady is married to Pastor Malcolm Jefferson where she supports his leadership and vision.

Printed in the United States
By Bookmasters